my first Nature BOOK

ARCTURUS

ARCTURUS

This edition published in 2021 by Arcturus Publishing Limited
26/27 Bickels Yard, 151–153 Bermondsey Street,
London SE1 3HA

Illustrator: Samantha Meredith
Author: Jacqueline McCann
Consultant: Helen Lewis
Designer: Ms Mousepenny

ISBN: 978-1-78950-315-9
CH007016UK
Supplier 33, Date 0921, Print run 12032

Printed in China

Living Things

Plants and animals are living things. All living things do three things—they move, grow, and reproduce.

Living things grow.

Animals have young. This baby orangutan will grow up to look like its parents.

Plants can move parts of themselves. Some flowers close up at night.

Plants make seeds that grow into new plants. This seedling will grow into a tree.

Animals can move around.

3

Plants Everywhere

Plants are living things with green parts. Most plants have leaves. They are found all over the Earth—even near the South Pole.

Some plants, such as trees, are very, very big.

These are plants you might see in the city.

plane tree

beech tree

grass

Other plants are very, very small.

moss

daffodils

grass

dandelion

4

Where Do I Grow?

A habitat is a place where a plant or animal lives naturally. Can you match each plant to the place where you think it grows?

poppy

cactus

fern

coconut palm

woodland

meadow

hot island

desert

Plant Parts

Plants are made of different parts. Lots of plants have flowers. It's the flowers that make seeds!

A sunflower

Most flowers have bright petals, to attract insects.

The flower makes seeds, which grow into new plants.

Leaves soak up light and heat from the Sun, to make food.

The stem supports the plant, and carries water and nutrients from the soil around the plant.

Roots are shoots that anchor the plant in the ground and take in water and nutrients too.

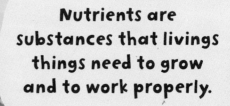

Nutrients are substances that livings things need to grow and to work properly.

Sunflowers face the Sun. They turn toward the Sun as it moves across the sky.

What Am I?

Read the captions and match them to the different parts of the plant.

We use light and heat to make food.

We hold the plant in the ground.

We attract insects.

We soak up water from the soil.

I carry water from the ground around the plant.

We help to make new plants.

We make seeds.

seeds

flower

petal

leaf

stem

roots

How Plants Grow

All plants need water, heat, and light from the Sun, plus nutrients from soil, to grow.

Light

Plants cannot grow in a dark place. They need light from the Sun.

Time

It takes many years for a tree to grow!

Warmth

Plants grow best when it is warm. They get heat from the Sun.

Air

Plants need to breathe, just like you!

Fungi

Mushrooms and other fungi help tree roots to absorb nutrients from the soil.

Water

Trees and other plants take in water from the soil through their roots.

Help Me Grow!

What does this little tomato plant need to help it grow? What are the things it does not need?

1 soil

2 butterfly

3 blackbird

4 sunshine

5 trowel

tomato

6 carton of milk

7 horse

Mighty Trees

Trees come in all shapes and sizes, and they can live for a very long time—even thousands of years. Most trees have flowers, but not all.

Some trees keep their leaves all year round. These are evergreen trees. The giant redwood is an evergreen.

Some trees lose their leaves in winter. These are called deciduous trees. The oak tree is deciduous.

Evergreen trees often have very thin leaves called needles. The fruit of the redwood is called a cone. When it opens, seeds are released.

Deciduous trees often have broad, green leaves. The fruit of the oak tree is a nut called an acorn. It has a seed inside.

Falling Leaves

Look closely at the leaves. Can you tell which ones come from deciduous trees, and which ones come from evergreen trees?

maple

Scots pine

ash

monkey puzzle

yew

ginkgo

horse chestnut

Lebanese cedar

Super Seeds

Most plants reproduce by making seeds. Some seeds fall from their parents and land close by, then they take root and grow. Other seeds are blown away by the wind. Animals and birds also pick up seeds and carry them far away.

The seed of the horse chestnut tree is inside the conker shell.

Some fruits have seeds inside. Birds eat the fruit and fly away. Later, they pass the seeds out in their poop! The seeds land and grow into new plants.

The seed of the sycamore tree is carried away on the wind. It twists and spins in the air, landing far from the parent tree.

The seed falls from the tree and lands on the ground below.

The seed grows into a seedling, which eventually grows into a new horse chestnut tree!

Dandelion seeds blow away in the wind, and grow into new dandelions far away.

From Seed to Plant

Can you figure out which seed grows into which plant? Follow the dotted lines to find out.

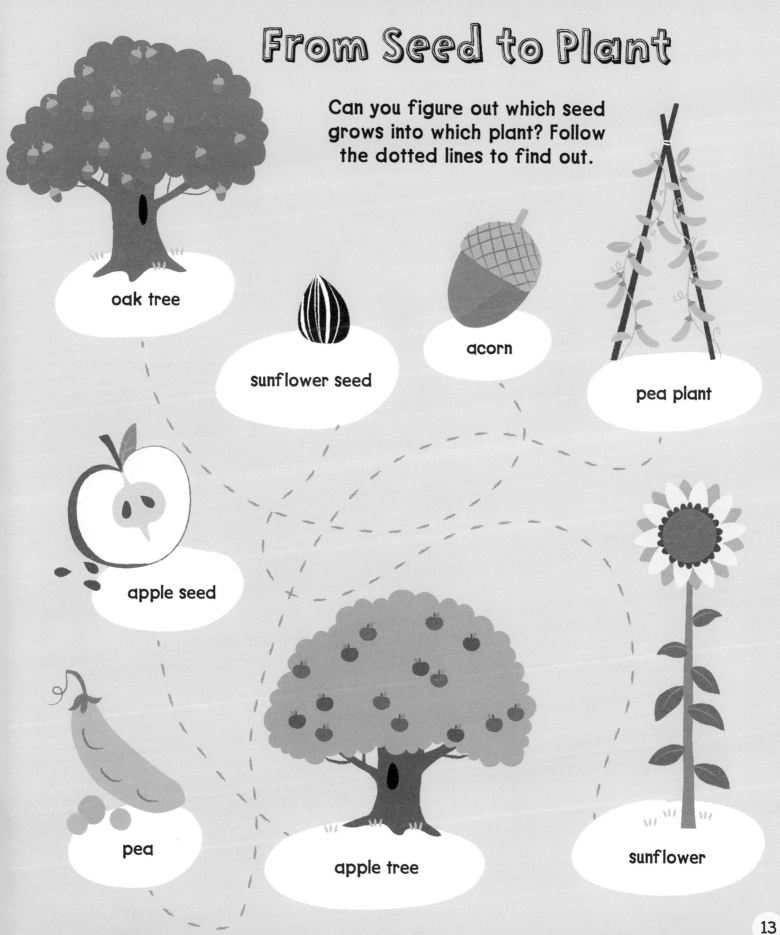

oak tree

sunflower seed

acorn

pea plant

apple seed

pea

apple tree

sunflower

Animal Kingdom

There are all kinds of incredible animals living on the planet. Scientists divide animals into two main groups—animals with backbones and animals without backbones.

Invertebrates are animals that don't have a backbone.

A beetle belongs to the insect famiy.

A spider is an arachnid.

Worms are some of the most common invertebrates.

A snail is a kind of mollusk.

A crab is a crustacean.

An octopus is a mollusk.

Vertebrates are animals that do have a backbone.

A turtle is a reptile.

A frog is an amphibian.

A rook is a bird.

A salamander is an amphibian.

A giraffe is a mammal.

A carp is a fish.

Human beings are mammals. Dogs are mammals too.

Rumble in the Jungle

All of these animals belong to one of the groups at the bottom of the page. Can you place each animal in the right group?

human

sloth

squirrel monkey

toucan

leopard

howler monkey

giant marauder ant

caiman

smoky jungle frog

poison arrow frog

discus fish

catfish

Insects have 6 legs.

Spiders have 8 legs.

Mollusks are animals with soft bodies. Most molluscs have shells.

Fish have wet scales and lay eggs in water.

wandering spider

red ants

parrot

tanager

tree boa

giant snail

horn snail

turtle

anteater

beetle

tree frog

chameleon

tarantula

apple snail

bird-eating spider

Birds have wings and feathers. They lay eggs.

Amphibians have moist skin and lay eggs in water.

Mammals have hair or fur. They have warm bodies. They feed their babies milk.

Reptiles have dry scales. Some reptiles have shells.

Beautiful Birds

All birds have feathers,
wings, two legs, and a beak.
They all lay eggs.
Most birds can fly!

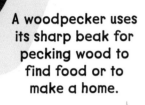

A woodpecker uses
its sharp beak for
pecking wood to
find food or to
make a home.

An eagle catches food
with its sharp talons.

A peacock spreads
its beautiful tail
feathers to attract
a peahen.

A duck has webbed
feet to paddle in water.

The kingfisher has strong, light feathers,
which are perfect for flying and diving.

Perfectly Suited

Birds are adapted to the places where they live and the food they need to catch. Look at the pictures below and find the correct word to complete each sentence opposite.

fish

nuts

rabbits

telephone wires

the sea

1 Penguins have webbed feet to help them swim in ...

2 Gannets have long, thin, jagged beaks, great for catching slippery ...

3 Bald eagles have huge talons adapted to catch fish and furry ...

4 Macaws have sharp, hooked bills, to help them crack hard ...

5 Swallows have tiny feet, ideal for gripping thin branches, or ...

Fishy Business

All fish have fins and their bodies are covered with wet scales. Fish cannot breathe air the way you do. They take in oxygen from the water, instead. Most fish live in the sea, which is salty. Some fish prefer freshwater rivers and lakes.

swordfish

Many fish live on or around coral reefs.

lionfish

Some fish live in large groups called shoals. They live in the open ocean.

shoal of mackerel

seahorse

angel fish

frilled shark

viperfish

angler fish

tripod fish

The bottom of the ocean is a very dark place, but fish do live there. Some fish can make light by themselves.

Sea Food

There are food chains in the sea as well as on land. Look at these animals. Can you place them in size order, showing which one eats the next?

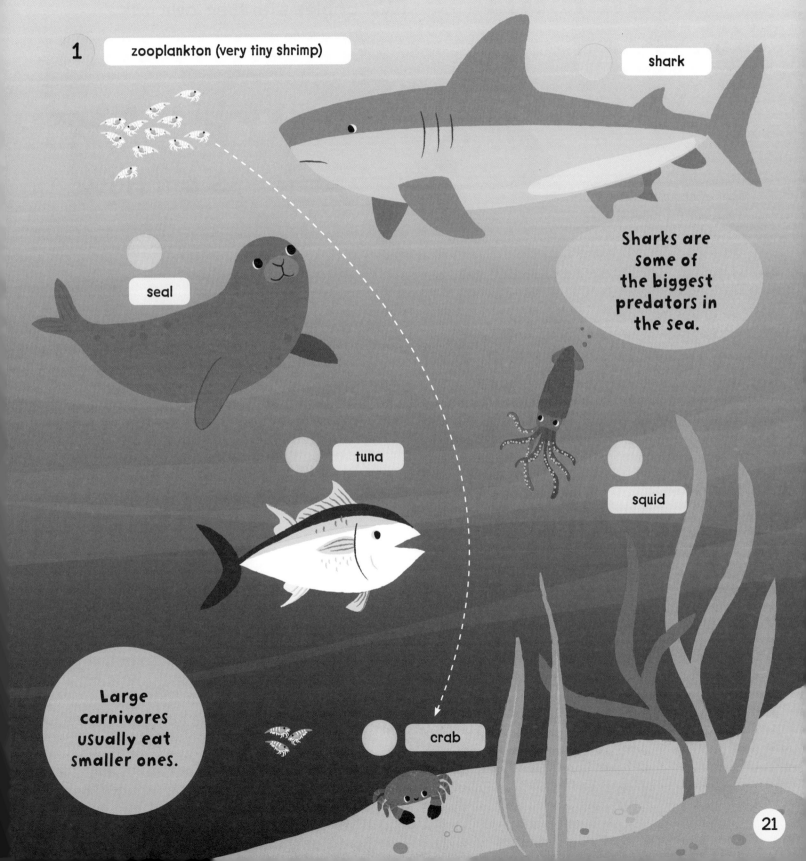

1 zooplankton (very tiny shrimp)

shark

seal

Sharks are some of the biggest predators in the sea.

tuna

squid

Large carnivores usually eat smaller ones.

crab

Mighty Mammals

Mammals have hair or fur (and sometimes prickles), and feed their babies with their own milk.

The porcupine has a coat of spiky prickles to protect it against predators.

Human beings are mammals. Most people have lots of hair on their head.

A tiger's stripy fur helps it to hide in long grass.

The echidna has fur and spiky spines to protect itself. It's a very rare mammal that lays eggs.

A dolphin is a mammal that lives in water. Dolphins are born with hair, but it drops out.

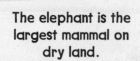

A mouse is a very small mammal with fur and a long tail.

The elephant is the largest mammal on dry land.

Find the Baby

These mothers have lost
their babies. Can you help
them find each other?

calf

goat

baby

bear

pinkie

human

joey

pup

camel

mouse

cub

seal

kid

kangaroo

ANSWERS

PAGE 5: Where Do I Grow?

Meadow: poppy
Hot island: coconut palm
Desert: cactus
Woodland: ferns

PAGE 7: What Am I?

We hold the plant in the ground: roots.

We soak up water from the soil: roots.

We help to make new plants: flower.

We use light and heat to make food: leaves.

We make seeds: flower.

We attract insects: flower.

I carry water up from the ground to the plant: stem.

PAGE 9: Help Me Grow!

The plant needs soil and sunshine.

PAGE 11: Falling Leaves

Deciduous: maple, horse chestnut, ash, ginkgo

Evergreen: Scots pine, monkey puzzle, yew, Lebanese cedar

PAGE 13: From Seed to Plant

PAGE 16-17: Rumble in the Jungle

Insects: red ants, giant marauder ant, beetle

Spiders: tarantula, wandering spider, bird-eating spider

Molluscs: giant snail, horn snail, apple snail

Fish: catfish, discus fish

Birds: toucan, tanager, parrot

Amphibians: tree frog, poison arrow frog, smoky jungle frog

Mammals: human, sloth, squirrel monkey, leopard, howler monkey, anteater

Reptiles: turtle, caiman, chameleon, tree boa

PAGE 19: Perfectly Suited

Gannets have long, thin, jagged beaks, great for catching slippery fish.

Bald eagles have huge talons adapted to catch fish and furry rabbits.

Penguins have webbed feet to help them swim in the sea.

Macaws have sharp, hooked bills, to help them crack hard nuts.

Swallows have tiny feet, ideal for gripping thin branches, or telephone wires.

PAGE 21: Sea Food

1. Zooplankton
2. Crab
3. Squid
4. Tuna
5. Seal
6. Shark

PAGE 23: Find the Baby

Human—baby
Bear—cub
Camel—calf
Goat—kid
Kangaroo—joey
Mouse—pinkie
Seal—pup